P9-DEY-524

Protoceratops

Written by Rupert Oliver
Illustrated by Roger Payne

Library of Congress Cataloging in Publication Data

Oliver, Rupert.
  Protoceratops.

  Summary: Follows Protoceratops through her day as she lays a batch of eggs, fights to defend the nest, and hides from fiercer dinosaurs.
  1. Protoceratops—Juvenile literature.
[1. Protoceratops.   2. Dinosaurs]   I. Title.
QE862.065O47   1985   567.9'7   85-19395
ISBN 0-86592-216-0

Rourke Enterprises, Inc.
Vero Beach, FL 32964

Dimorphodon

Brachiosaurus

Dilophosaurus

Lystrosaurus

Rutiodon

Protoceratops

Mamenchisaurus

Plateosaurus

Chasmosaurus

Protoceratops

The long neck of Nemegtosaurus curved gracefully up to the branches. The small teeth took a small mouthful of leaves from the topmost branches which were swallowed instantly and another mouthful taken. The lower branches were being stripped of their greenery by a pair of Opisthocoelicaudia.

A quiet shuffling noise caused Nemegtosaurus to look down toward his feet. Brushing past him through the clearing was a small, four legged dinosaur. The small Protoceratops was no threat to the giant Sauropods and they continued to eat.

Protoceratops pushed on through the forest. She was looking for a place to lay her eggs. The tough undergrowth of the forest was quite unsuitable for it would not shelter her eggs. Protoceratops was looking for some loose earth in which she could bury her eggs.

Nosing through the greenery of the palms, Protoceratops found herself by the banks of a river. The sloping banks were covered with sand and Protoceratops began to dig. When she had dug out a round hole, Protoceratops laid her eighteen eggs in three concentric circles. Then she brushed the sand back over the eggs. Having finished such hard work, Protoceratops was thirsty and she walked down to the river to drink.

No sooner had Protoceratops taken her first mouthful of water, than she heard a scrabbling noise behind her. Turning around she saw an Oviraptor digging up her eggs. Protoceratops knew that Oviraptor liked to eat eggs. She would have to protect her unhatched young somehow.

Lowering her head so as to present the hard bony frill to Oviraptor, Protoceratops charged forward. Oviraptor looked up. He fell back before the charging Protoceratops, then turned and ran away. Protoceratops was so angry that she did not stop when Oviraptor retreated. She continued to chase him blindly through the undergrowth, trampling plants beneath her thundering feet.

Suddenly Protoceratops emerged from the forest into the bright sunlight of a clearing. She stopped in fear. Right in front of her was a pack of Velociraptors. She knew how dangerous these dinosaurs could be, with the huge claws on their hind feet. Luckily the Velociraptors had not seen Protoceratops. They seemed to be watching something else. Quietly, Protoceratops backed into the foliage, hoping she would not be noticed.

The object of the Velociraptors' attention came into sight. It was a Homalocephale. As soon as the Homalocephale saw the Velociraptors it turned and fled. The pack of Velociraptors roared in excitement and plunged after their prey. As they disappeared from sight, Protoceratops moved back into the undergrowth.

As Protoceratops moved through the trees she
became aware of two large animals nearby. They
were eating the shoots and fruits of the bushes. The
large Nodosaurs turned and looked at Protoceratops
before continuing to feed.

Protoceratops suddenly realized just how hungry she was herself. She found a clump of low palms and began to slice off the spiky leaves with her sharp teeth. Whenever she bit through a stem the sweet, milky sap of the palm would ooze out. Protoceratops lapped the sap up hungrily, it was her favorite part of the plant.

After eating her fill of the palm plant and licking up the sap, Protoceratops was no longer hungry. It was then that she sensed something was wrong. She was not near her eggs and they might be in danger. Quickly she hurried through the trees to the river bank where she had laid her eggs. Thankfully nothing had happened to her nest. The sand was undisturbed and the eggs were safe. Protoceratops knew that until the eggs were hatched she would have to stay close to the riverbank to protect the nest.

A large drop of water fell on Protoceratops' nose, causing her to shake her head. Then more drops fell all around and the trees began to sway as the wind became stronger. Protoceratops crouched under a bush as the rain fell more heavily and the wind grew stronger.

A bright flash of lightning streaked across the sky and a deep rumble of thunder boomed through the forest. Protoceratops huddled lower in fear. The rain was falling in torrents from the dark sky and the trees were twisting and lurching in the violent storm.

Heavy footsteps sounded from the trees and a huge Tarbosaurus ran from the forest toward the river. It had been frightened by the storm and was running in sheer panic. Just as the large dinosaur reached the river bank a bolt of lightning flashed down from the sky and struck the Tarbosaurus. The huge beast twisted in pain and then crashed to the ground. It lay still and did not move.

In time the storm passed and the sun came out. A Chingkankousaurus and a pair of Velociraptors came to scavenge food from the dead Tarbosaurus. Protoceratops did not dare move when such fierce meat eaters were nearby. She stayed huddled under the bushes. Evening was drawing on now and perhaps the hunters would leave when night came. Then Protoceratops could move out and eat some more palms and continue to keep an eye on her nest. One day soon her young would hatch.

Protoceratops and Late Cretaceous Asia

Skull of Protoceratops

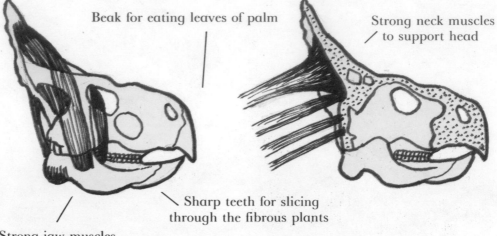

Beak for eating leaves of palm

Strong neck muscles to support head

Sharp teeth for slicing through the fibrous plants

Strong jaw muscles

When Protoceratops lived

Life in one form or another has existed on Earth for many hundreds of millions of years. Living beings have existed during the past 570 million years and scientists have divided this immense stretch of time into three eras. The earliest was the Paleozoic, the second was the Mesozoic, and the third, the Cenozoic. The Mesozoic is often known as the age of the dinosaurs and began 225 million years ago and ended 65 million years ago. It is divided into three periods: the Triassic, the Jurassic and the Cretaceous. Protoceratops lived near the end of the third period, the Cretaceous. This means it was alive about 75 million years ago.

Where Protoceratops lived

The fossils of Protoceratops have been found in rocks deep in the heart of the Gobi Desert. This great tract of barren land lies in Mongolia, in central Asia. Today the Gobi is cold and inhospitable but when Protoceratops roamed the region, the land was lush with plant life and animals. Many of the plants of the time would seem strangely familiar today. There were magnolias, conifers, ferns, oak trees and palms growing in profusion. The most important aspect of the plant life of the time was the appearance of flowering plants. Such plants had only been

on earth for a few million years when Protoceratops lived, but they were already the commonest plants and remain so to this day.

Lifestyle of Protoceratops

Protoceratops was a relatively small dinosaur. It was only about 6 feet long, but at the same time it was very heavily built. It therefore faced two problems of survival. Being small, it was easily hunted, and being heavy, it found running difficult. It managed to survive because of the bony armor of its head and perhaps by hiding in the forests. It certainly needed to stay close to palms for it would appear that these were its favorite food. Many Protoceratops' nests, similar to the one in the story, have been found by scientists. In common with other dinosaurs, Protoceratops probably looked after the nest and may even have cared for her young after they hatched.

Family tree of Protoceratops

Protoceratops was the earliest known member of a family of dinosaurs called Ceratopsians. All members of the family had the heavy build and bony head frill of the Protoceratops. Over the next few million years the Ceratopsians evolved into larger and larger forms and many sprouted huge, dangerous horns. The most famous of all

Ceratopsians is probably Triceratops. Triceratops was 30 feet long, weighed six tons and had three large horns. The Ceratopsian family continued to evolve and to become more numerous until they suddenly died out about 65 million years ago. At the same time all other dinosaurs died out, together with the pterosaurs and sea reptiles.

Animals of late Cretaceous Asia

The rocks of the Gobi Desert are rich in fossils and from these, scientists can tell which animals lived together with Protoceratops. Some of these animals appear in our story. Nemegtosaurus and Opisthocoelicaudia both belonged to a dinosaur family called Sauropod. These were the largest dinosaurs of all, but by the time of Protoceratops they were becoming much rarer than they had been. At the same time many new types of dinosaurs were appearing. Oviraptor is one of these dinosaurs. The family to which this egg stealer belonged did not appear until the time of Protoceratops. A slightly older family was that of

the Dromaeosaurs, to which Velociraptor belonged. The family is distinguished by a large claw on the hind feet with which the animals were able to hunt ferociously. It was with good reason that Protoceratops was afraid of Velociraptor. The Nodosaur family first appeared at about the same time as the Dromaeosaurs. Nodosaurus itself was a huge beast some 18 feet long, but in time the family would produce even larger plant eaters. The largest meat eater of the time was the powerful Tarbosaurus. This huge beast was about 45 feet long and was probably the mightiest hunter of the period. Chingkankousaurus was much smaller than Tarbosaurus, but may have been more agile and therefore more dangerous to such animals as Protoceratops. However, it was not just dinosaurs which stalked the land so many millions of years ago. There were many other sorts of reptiles, including lizards, tortoises and snakes, together with amphibians and some mammals. Today mammals are the most important group of animals on earth. Man himself is a mammal and so are most of the large animals which live on land. During the times of Protoceratops, however, mammals were small and unimportant.

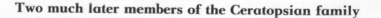

Two much later members of the Ceratopsian family

Triceratops

Styracosaurus

	DATE DUE		
Hicks			
Sta-			

567.9   Oliver, Rupert   c.1
O   Protoceratops